Rookie
Read-About® Science

What Is Volume?

By Lisa Trumbauer

Subject Consultant
Andrew Fraknoi
Chair, Astronomy Program
Foothill College
Los Altos Hills, California

Reading Consultant
Cecilia Minden-Cupp, PhD
Former Director of the Language and Literacy Program
Harvard Graduate School of Education
Cambridge, Massachusetts

Children's Press®
A Division of Scholastic Inc.
New York   Toronto   London   Auckland   Sydney
Mexico City   New Delhi   Hong Kong
Danbury, Connecticut

Designer: Herman Adler Design
Photo Researcher: Caroline Anderson
The photo on the cover shows a measuring cup filled with crayons.

Library of Congress Cataloging-in-Publication Data

Trumbauer, Lisa, 1963–
  What is volume? / by Lisa Trumbauer; consultants, Andrew Fraknoi,
Cecilia Minden-Cupp.
      p. cm. — (Rookie Read-About Science)
  Includes index.
  ISBN 0-516-23621-0 (lib. bdg.)   0-516-24661-5 (pbk.)
  1. Weights and measures—Juvenile literature. 2. Volume—Juvenile
literature. I. Title. II. Series.
  QC90.6.T788 2006
  530.8'1—dc22   2005021736

CHILDREN'S PRESS, and ROOKIE READ-ABOUT®,
and associated logos are trademarks and/or registered trademarks
of Scholastic Library Publishing. SCHOLASTIC and associated logos
are trademarks and/or registered trademarks of Scholastic Inc.

4 5 6 7 8 9 10 R 15 14 13 12 11 10 09   62

Would you like to cook
something new?

First, you need a recipe. Recipes tell you how much food you will need. You might read words such as teaspoon and tablespoon and cup.

Teaspoons, tablespoons, and cups measure how much space something takes up.

Everything takes up space.
How we measure that
space is called volume.

Have you ever bought a pint of ice cream?

A pint is a measurement of volume. Two cups equal one pint.

Two pints equal one quart.
How many cups do you
think are in one quart?

If you said four, you are
right! Four cups equal
one quart.

Four quarts equal one gallon.

Have you ever tried to
carry a gallon of milk?
A gallon of milk is heavy!

Volume is not the same as weight. It does not tell you how heavy something is. Ounces and pounds measure weight.

Milk, marbles, and feathers take up space. They can have the same volume. Do you think they have the same weight?

You could fill a gallon jug with milk, with marbles, or with feathers. They would take up the same space. They would have the same volume. But they would not weigh the same!

18

Have you seen a container like this before? It is called a liter.

A liter is another way to measure volume. Liters are part of the metric system. The metric system is another way to measure things.

Teaspoons, tablespoons, and cups measure liquid volume. Pints, quarts, and gallons measure liquid volume. Liters measure liquid volume, too.

Do solid things have volume?
Yes, they do. You can
measure their volume, too!

22

These cubes are one inch on every side. Each cube takes up one cubic inch of space. Cubic inches are one way to measure the volume of a solid.

Fill the box to the top with one-inch cubes. This box can hold thirty-two cubes. The volume of the box is 32 cubic inches.

Here is a box shaped like a rectangle. What do you think the volume of this box is? Let's use the cubes to find out.

Fill the box with the cubes.
Seventy cubes fit inside.
The volume of this box is
70 cubic inches.

Liquid objects take up space. Solid objects take up space, too. We know how much space they take up by measuring volume.

How much space do you take up?

Words You Know

cup

gallon

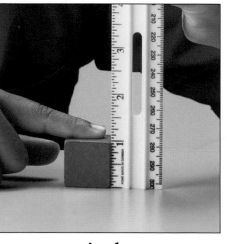

inch

liter

pint

quart

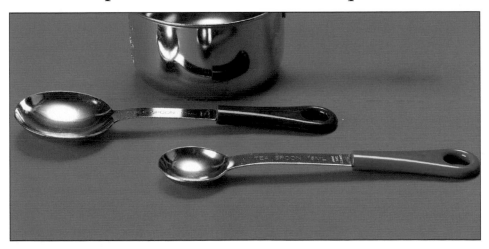

tablespoon   teaspoon

Index

About the Author

Lisa Trumbauer is the author of more than two hundred books for children, many of which are science related. Formerly an editor with Scientific American Library Books, Lisa went on to edit several science programs for early learners. In addition, she has written science books about animals, plants, the Earth, and the physical sciences. Lisa and her husband, Dave, live in New Jersey with their dog, Blue, and their cats, Cosmo and Cleo.

Photo Credits